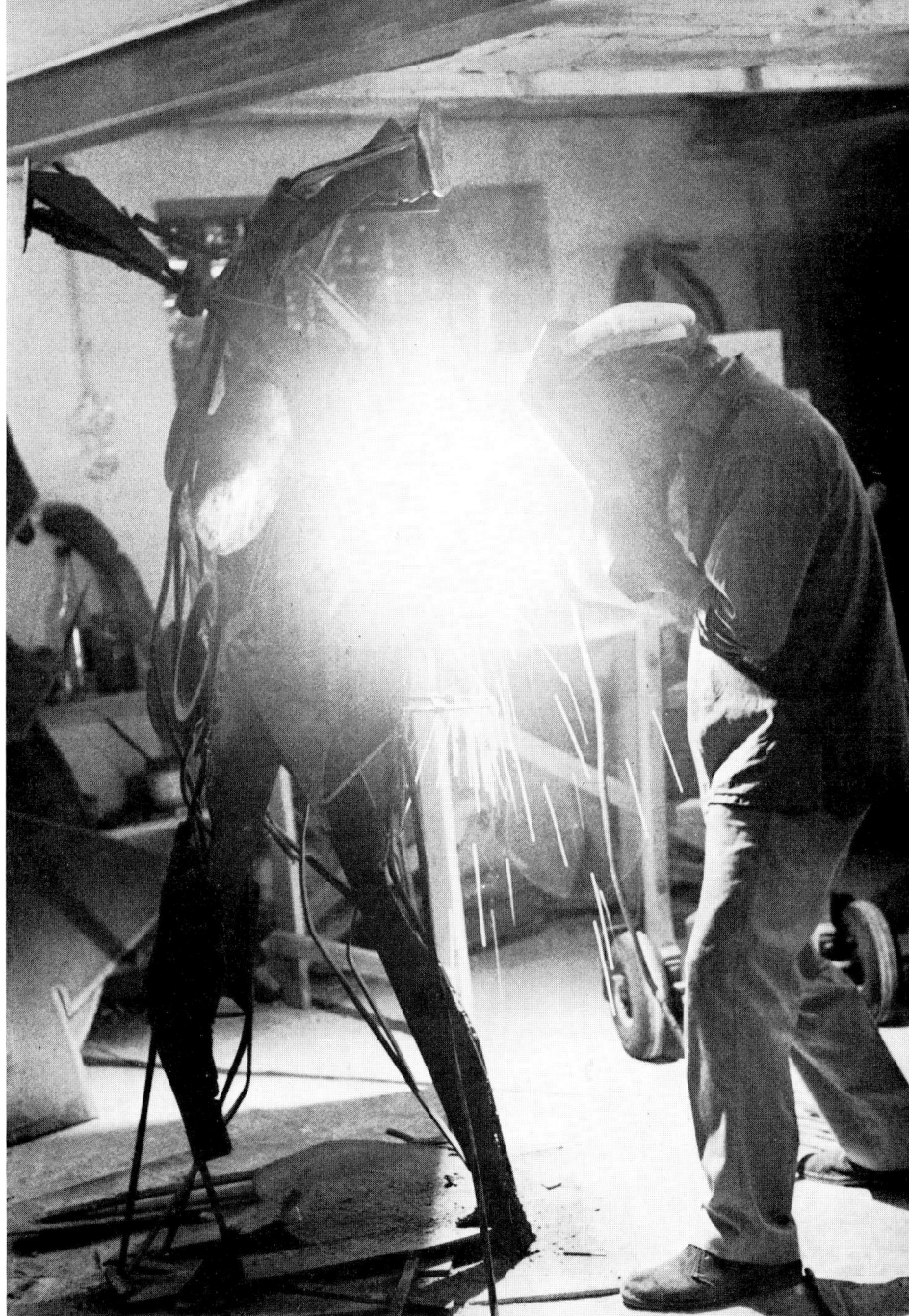

Bei der Arbeit am Eisen

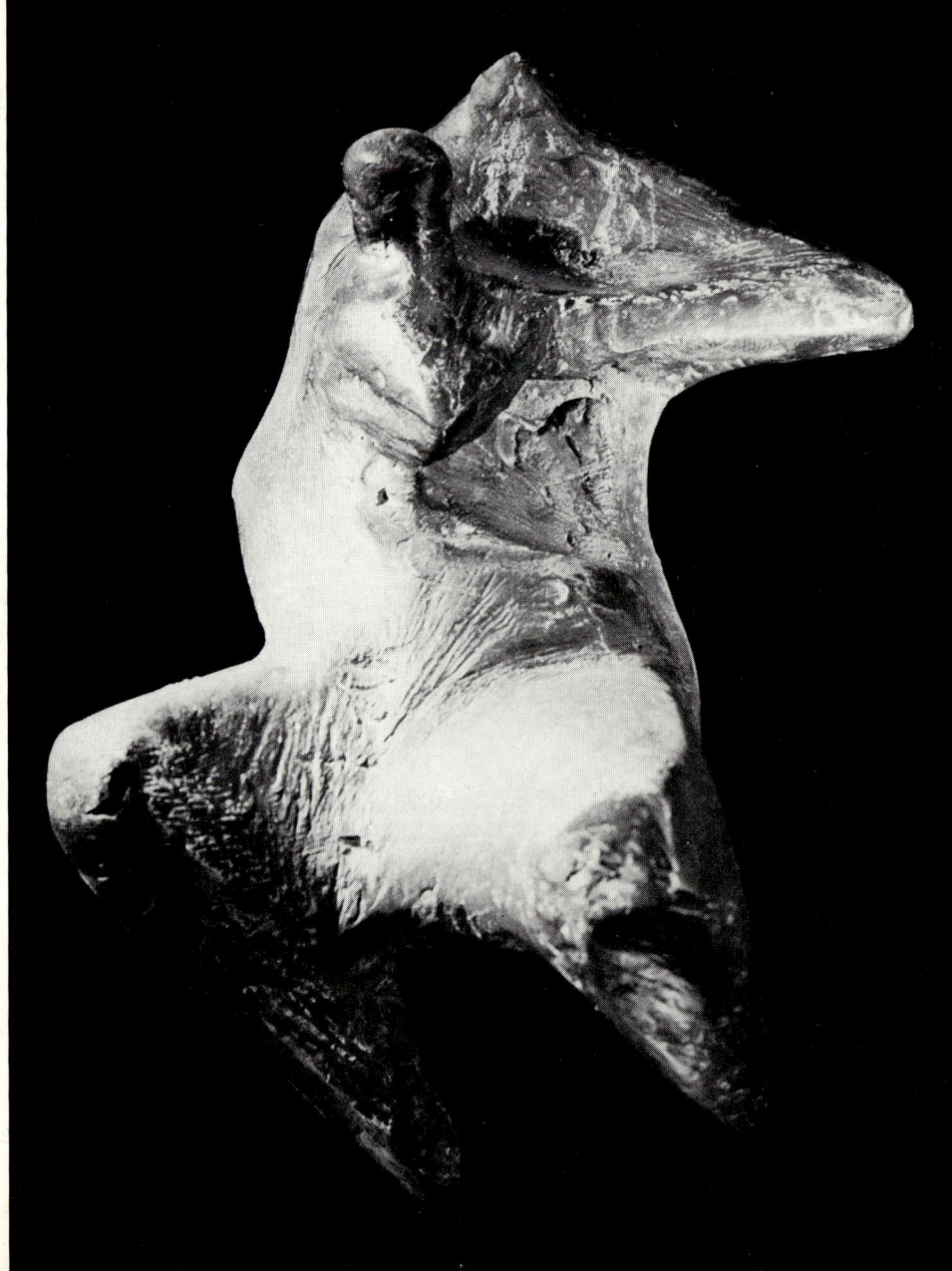

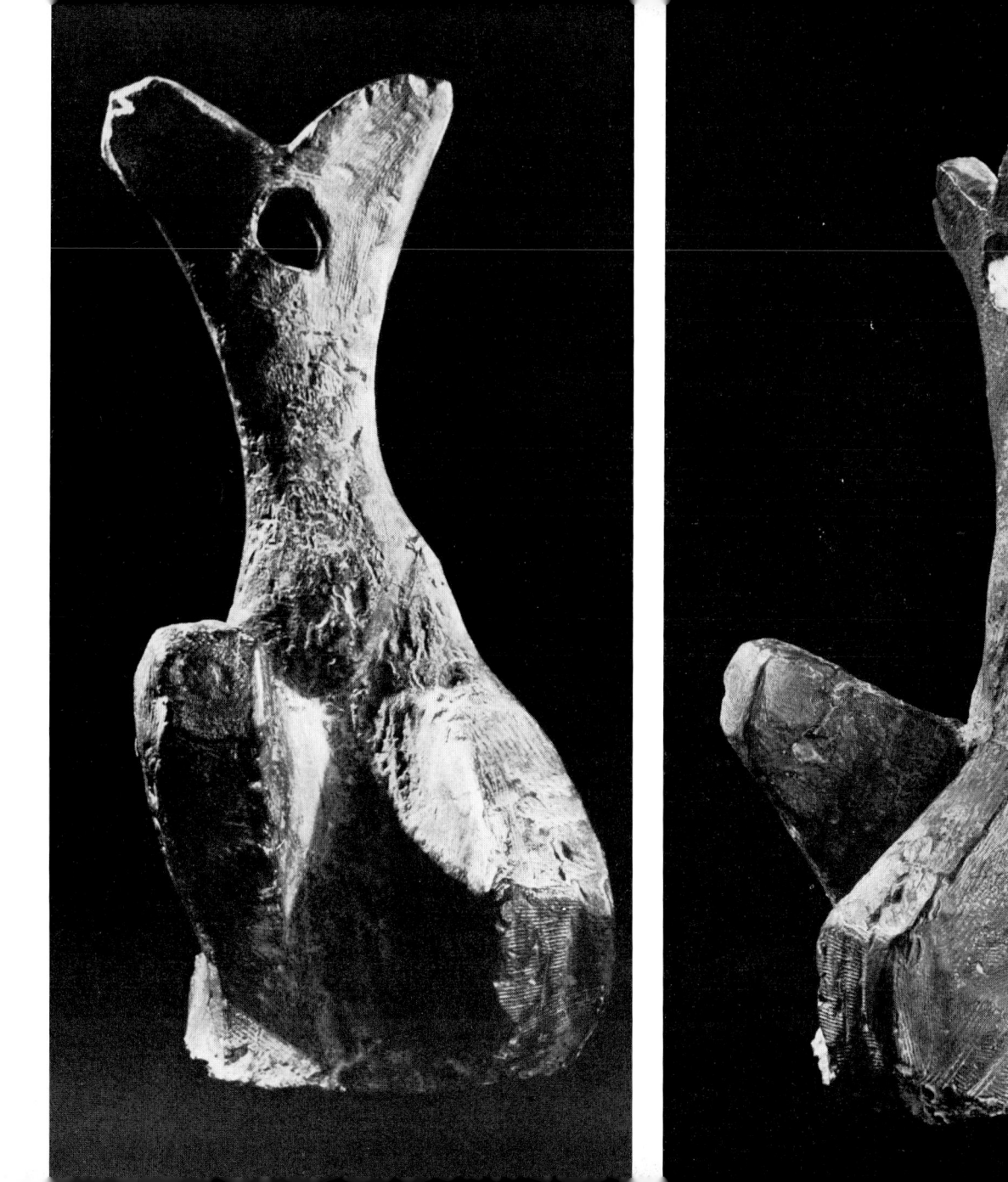

4

GUGLIELMO GIGLI, Venezia   in »Quadrante delle arti« Napoli

Das Schaffen Oldenburgs ist breit, ausladend, es schöpft aus vielen Quellen. Von den Plastiken aus verschiedenen Materialien erstreckt es sich bis zur Grafik und den Ölgemälden. Alles läßt sich aber auf ein einzigartiges Gefühl für die Kunst und den Menschen zurückführen, zwei Komponente, die sich in ihm „monumental" verdichten, die groß, bedeutend und unersetzbar sind.
Der Mensch ist für Oldenburg nicht nur ein Vorwand für eine gültige ästhetische Form; er ist die einzige Möglichkeit zum eigenen Wesen der Kunst vorzudringen. Eine Form, die ohne menschliche Präsenz für Oldenburg nur zu einem reinen Spiel der Fantasie oder der Geschicklichkeit würde, aber kein Bild, keine Plastik ergäbe. Und so geht es um den Menschen in der fortdauernden Suche nach der Kunst, dem sich Oldenburg früher und heute in erster Linie mit Hingabe widmet, beinahe mit einer „Angst", die Zeit

L'opera di Oldenburg è ampia, vastissima, eclettica. Va dalle sculture nei materiali più diversi alla grafica ed alla pittura ad olio. Tutto, però, è sempre riportato ad

Oldenburg's works are vast and cover a wide range; they are created from many sources. From sculptures of diversified material they extend through graphic work and oil paintings. All of this can be attributed to a unique feeling for art and humanity, two components which have taken hold of him in a monumental way; these are great, significant and irreplaceable.
Man is for Oldenburg not only an excuse for a valid aesthetic form; he is the only possibility through which art's essential being can be reached. A form without human presence would, as far as Oldenburg is concerned, only result in a pure play of fantasy or ability - but in no image or sculpture. And so it has to do primarily with a devotion to people to which Oldenburg has dedicated himself almost with a „fear" that time itself will not suffice to express all that he feels.
Then sculpturing in stone and

könne nicht reichen, all das auszusagen, was er fühlt.
Dann die Bildhauerei, in Stein und Eisen - eine schwierige Aufgabe, mühsam, zeitraubend - jene Zeit von der Oldenburg fürchtet, sie könne nicht genügen ihm zu gestatten, sich ganz mitzuteilen.
In der Weite des Hofes hinter seinem Hause stehen in einer Art Dauerausstellung die großen Werke

Oldenburgs. Für jeden, der vorübergeht oder der sie bewußt

un unico sentimento verso l'arte e verso l'uomo che sono due poesie, in lui, «monumentali», cioè grandi, importanti, insostituibili. L'uomo di Oldenburg non è solo pretesto per una forma esteticamente valida: è l'unica possibilità per raggiungere l'arte stessa. Una forma che non avesse la sostanza della presenza umana sarebbe, per Oldenburg, un puro gioco di fantasia o di abilità, non un quadro od una scultura. E attorno a quest' uomo, alla ricerca continua dell'arte, Oldenburg ha lavorato e lavora con un impegno che è, prima di ogni altra cosa, «ansia», paura di non arrivare a dire tutto ciò che ha dentro. La scultura su pietra ed in ferro, poi, è cosa difficile, faticosa, e si porta via del tempo; quel tempo che Oldenburg teme non sia sufficiente a permettergli di esprimersi tutto.
Nell'ampio spazio a fianco della sua casa, in una sorta di mostra permanente per chi vi passa davanti o la cerca, le grandi opere di Oldenburg rappresentano i momenti di un racconto plastico che prosegue per immagini, caratterizzanti situazioni generali

iron - a difficult undertaking, toilsome, time-consuming - exactly that time which Oldenburg fears will not suffice to completely express himself.
In the expanse of the yard behind his house stand the great works of Oldenburg - in a kind of permanent display. For those who either in transition or in a state of awareness are able to observe, they represent the passing

wahrnimmt, stellen sie die Augenblicke einer plastischen Erzählung dar, die in fortschreitenden Bildern immer wieder die generellen Begebenheiten im Leben des Menschen charakterisiert. In den Plastiken und Gemälden dieses Deutschen drückt sich ständig die Suche nach der Idealisierung des menschlichen Lebens aus, die Sublimierung jedes Augenblicks, auch des dramatischsten. Denn Oldenburg gibt seinen Figuren immer dramatische und lebendige Spannung. Jedes seiner Werke gibt uns zu denken, erschüttert und stimuliert uns, erweckt in uns Gedanken und Empfindungen, eben weil aus der scheinbaren Einfachheit der Formen Impulse auftauchen: Mahnungen, die verletzen und ergreifen können. Die grandiose Gesamtkonzeption, die der menschlichen Gestalt eine fast „michelangolisch" anmutende Großartigkeit verleiht, die noch unterstrichen wird durch die von ihm am häufigsten gewählten Materialien: ein besonders roher, poröser Stein, der nicht viele Rundungen und Spielereien mit dem Licht gestattet, sondern sich nur

della vita dell'uomo. C'è, insomma, nelle sculture e pitture del tedesco, la ricerca di idealizzazione della vita dell'uomo, di sublimazione di ogni suo momento, anche del più drammatico. Perché Oldenburg dà ai suoi personaggi una tensione sempre drammatica e viva; ogni sua opera fa pensare, scuote, eccita, stimola riflessioni e sensazioni, proprio perché dalla apparente semplicità delle forme emergono

moments of a sculptural narrative which always characterizes - again and again in progressive images - the general affairs in the life of Man. The paintings and sulptures of this German express the constant search for the idealization of human life, the sublime in every moment, even the most dramatic. For Oldenburg always lends his figures dramatic and living tension Each of his works makes us think,

durch plastische Lösungen einer außerordentlich schaffenden In-

telligenz und durch eine äußerst ausdrucksvolle Empfindsamkeit gestalten läßt.
Darum ist Oldenburg „modern" und antik zugleich. Einerseits klassisch und andererseits ursprünglich. Immer aber lebendig und unerschöpflich in seiner kreativen Energie.

impulsi e suggerimenti che feriscono e graffiano.
La grandiosità della concezione, che dona alla figura umana una maestosità che oseremo dire «michelangiolesca», si accentua, inoltre, nell'uso del mezzo per più adoperato: una speciale pietra grezza, porosa, che non ammette il tutto tondo o la leziosità dei giochi di luce, ma si fa forma solo attraverso soluzioni plastiche di una estrema intelligenza creativa e di una efficacissima sensibilità espressiva. Oldenburg, pertanto, è «moderno» ed antico allo stesso tempo. Classico per un verso e primitivo per un altro. Sempre, però, vivo ed inesauribile nella sua vena creativa.

moves us deeply and stimulates us; awakens submerged sensitivities for the precise reason that out of the apparent simplicity of the forms, impulses surface: admonitions which can grip and hurt.
The grandiose total concept which lends an almos Michelangelo-like grace and splendor to the human form is even more so emphasized by the materials normally chosen by him: an especially rough, porous stone which does not tolerate many curves or play with light and shadow, but which only lets itself be shaped through the sculptural dénoument of an extra-ordinarily creative intelligence and a superbly expressive sensitivity.
Oldenburg is therefore at once „modern" and ancient. On the one hand classical and on the other original, yet always lively and indefatigueable in his creative energy.

Der Maler im Atelier

5